KV-684-829

RECOLLECTIONS

The Museum of Antiquities, for the past forty years the main museum for Hadrian's Wall, has an internationally famous collection of Roman antiquities. In 2009 the collection will be transferred to the Great North Museum. This volume uses the poetry of the Museum's poet-in-residence, Maureen Almond, and the photographs of the Museum's Audio Visual Officer, Glyn Goodrick, to celebrate the work and collections of the Museum and to explore the interconnections between the Romans and the modern museum visitor.

Lindsay Allason-Jones

Director of Archaeological Museums for Newcastle University

RECOLLECTIONS

Poems by Maureen Almond

Photographs by Glyn Goodrick

FlambardPress

In association with the
Museum of Antiquities of the University
and Society of Antiquaries of Newcastle upon Tyne

First published in Great Britain in 2008 by Flambard Press
Stable Cottage, East Fourstones, Hexham NE47 5DX
www.flambardpress.co.uk

Design, typesetting and artwork by Gainford Design Associates
Typeset in Albertus and Palatino
Cover photography by Glyn Goodrick
Printed in Great Britain by Statex, Newcastle upon Tyne

A CIP catalogue record for this book is available from the British Library

ISBN 978-1-873226-97-1

Book copyright © Flambard Press 2008
Poems copyright © Maureen Almond 2008
Photographs copyright © Glyn Goodrick
Foreword copyright © Richard Bailey

All rights reserved
Maureen Almond and Glyn Goodrick have asserted
their moral rights in accordance with the Copyright
Designs and Patents Act of 1988

Flambard Press wishes to thank Arts Council England
for its financial support

Flambard Press is a member of Inpress

FSC
Mixed Sources
Product group from well-managed
forests, controlled sources and
recycled wood or fiber

Cert no. SGS-COC-3058
www.fsc.org
© 1996 Forest Stewardship Council

Contents

Foreword

The story opens in 1813. In that year, a group of some seventy local gentlemen founded the Society of Antiquaries of Newcastle upon Tyne – the first such society in England outside London. Almost immediately they began to collect antiquities from across the north of England and, indeed, from further afield. Here lay the origins of the amazing collections which formed the Museum of Antiquities.

The Museum is now to be integrated with two other internationally significant collections – the Shefton and the Hancock – into the Great North Museum. This publication marks the transition, and does so in a very appropriate form because, although the collections have been constantly exploited by academics to understand our past, the Museum over the last few decades has been a national leader in developing wider audiences and drawing on its treasures for innovative projects.

One of the most successful of these projects has been to use the Museum as a stimulus for creative writing. In recent years, under Maureen Almond's tactful guidance, many adults have discovered within themselves a hitherto unsuspected ability to articulate their thoughtful and personal reflections on the archaeological objects in the Museum's galleries. In this volume Maureen herself responds to the stimulus of the Museum's Roman collection. Both her poetry and Glyn Goodrick's characteristically evocative photographs respond less to the objects themselves than to the soldiers and civilians who made, wore, used and even died with them in this frontier zone.

Fifty years ago, when television and archaeology were first realising that they had much to give each other, Sir Mortimer Wheeler wrote that 'the archaeological excavator is not digging up things; he is digging up people'. It is people – past and present – who are at the heart of Maureen Almond's poetry and of the Museum of Antiquities.

Emeritus Professor Richard Bailey
Chair of Joint Museum Committee

Best of Both Worlds

With fire-filled bellies we turned our native hand
to honing Latin customs in our land.

Our blood was spilt but we were never crushed,
we spoke your words, though ours were never hushed.

We watched you work your fingers to the bone,
we learned your skills but didn't lose our own.

Like Janus we're two-faced; one looked to Rome,
the other, wide-eyed, turned its gaze to home.

So when at last you left our British shores,
we kept the best of both worlds – ours and yours.

Dragonesque Brooch. Milking Gap, Nd. Bronze and enamel.
1st – 2nd century AD. 1938.34. Background: cup-and-ring decorated
cist cover. Doddington, Nd. Sandstone. Neolithic. 1909.4.19.

In Praise of Lead

A Roman Plumber's Prayer

I pour you out in sheets, Father of All Metals,
and don't believe you'll bring an empire down.
Shaped round cores of wood, you pipe a town,
duct fresh spring water to our baths and kettles.

I'll pay my dues to have a wider nozzle
then name you, as I set you into stone.
You, the vital vein, the city backbone,
because of you we put down roots and settle.

What's left, plebeian lead, I'll shape to vessels.
I'm accustomed to your sweetness in my wine.
Not Bacchus do I call, nor summon Vulcan,
but Saturn with his gout and all the hassle.

You sugar both our water and our wine.
I'll show them that this madness isn't mine.

Water pipe. Corbridge Red House, Nd. Lead. 2nd century AD.
1961.19.17. Photographed with bronze ewer from R. Tyne, Newcastle
upon Tyne, 3rd century AD. 1888.10, and pottery drinking vessel from
Carrawburgh Mithraeum, Nd. 4th century AD. 1956.128.18.

Mortarium. South Shields, T&W. Pottery. 2nd century AD. 1956.128.123.
Photographed with patera from Risingham, Nd. Bronze. 2nd century AD,
1925.1.27, and glass grinder from South Shields, T&W. 1956.128.14.

Recipe for Englishness

Take a couple of hundred Roman soldiers,
spice them up with notions of Empire,
add one Governor, sick for Rome,
sprinkle liberally with bargained pepper,
grind down in a mortarium, huge as a wall,
sweeten generously with honey and wine,
then set aside in an amphora
and cool to 1AD Northern climes.

After two months
add the rotting guts of several local wild boar,
a pinch of broken Celtic hearts,
some onion (for tears).
Stir well.

Pour into olive-oiled black-burnished bowls
and leave to set for two thousand years.

Spanish amphora. Turret 44B (Mucklebank), Nd. Pottery. 2nd century AD. 1904.11.

Amphora

Our taste for oil began with you.
We took you, fat-bellied and knocked
you into our home ground. We knew
you would fill us up so we flocked
around you, draining the last drop.

Years later and we want still more.
We pump the deserts of the world
to fatten our bellies. We're poured
onto troubled water and hurled
into battle till the last drop.

Drinking vessel. Clavering Place, Newcastle upon Tyne. Pottery.
3rd century AD. 1903.12. Background: Child's coffin. Clavering Place,
Newcastle upon Tyne. 3rd century AD. 1903.10.

The Cup

Nothing but an imprint in the sandstone,
a three-foot, four-inch profile of your life.
An extra rib suggests you'd be a wife,
had death not intervened before you'd grown,

and at your feet a cup, a vessel thrown
with love; its icing, baby finger marked;
a familiar thing to take back to the dark,
a keepsake, so you wouldn't feel alone.

It's difficult with the gap in time to grieve;
never to have touched you; not to have known
your voice. Impossible, almost, to believe
the winds that brushed your cheeks have blown
on ours. Is this what we can expect to leave;
a pattern, a loving cup, a hint of bone?

Erase

'Saepe stilum vertas'
(often must you turn your pencil to erase)
Horace: Satire 1.10.72

You may have a point
but scribble it down lightly
ready for smearing.

Pen. South Shields, T&W. Bronze. 2nd – 3rd century AD. 1956.128.33.

Antenociticus Speaks

You thank me for your promotion Tineius,
yet say nothing of my qualities as a god.

You happily attribute your broad stripe to me
with no mention of my special place in heaven.

You don't spell out how I kill the competition,
turn winners into failures; mess with minds.

You could have said how this innocent little god
can transform heroes into whimpering dogs.

As for horse control; I can make them throw a man
as easily as a shoe; yet of that you say nothing.

Your vow fulfilled, I wonder, will you return
to offer a thanksgiving at my altar?

Does it occur to you, we gods need constant praise,
mortals who will raise incantation and incense?

Head of Antenociticus. Benwell, T&W. Sandstone. 2nd century AD.
1924.8; Background: altar dedicated to Antenociticus by Tineius
Longus. Benwell. Sandstone. 2nd century AD. 1887.25

Intaglio. Hadrian's Wall. Onyx. 3rd century AD. 1962.13.

Cupid on a Prancing Horse

For months I've watched your gentle, caring hands,
our eyes have met yet not a word's been spoken.
I never dreamed you'd give me such a token,
and you a Roman doctor in strange lands.

I'll wear with pride your agate cupid band
and pass my days concocting love's sweet potion.
Anicius, our seal will not be broken,
and I'm impatient too – we must make plans.

Centurion I didn't think to fall
for such as you, but passion's arrow's flown,
so promise when time served, you leave the Wall,
you'll take your darling Pullia back to Rome,
or Syria, or Egypt or to Gaul,
for anywhere with you would be my home.

The Doctor of Housesteads

Anicius Ingenuus, medicus ordinarius

In this hilly place you were transformed;
grew inch by inch into your doctor's skin.
A Tungrian, in charge of bandagers;
what care had you for rank, Centurion?

Holder of some ancient hidden teaching,
who worked by intuition and alone;
you darted like a hare from wound to wound,
to cut along the mile of cragged whinstone.

In your hands, extraordinary powers;
though not for you, inscriptions on the wall,
just ink on wood reports of soldiers mended,
to fight again for Empire, then to fall.

Greek or Celt or Roman, it's no matter,
Anicius, you did what you could do.
A freeborn child; a former free(d)man's son.
We should have named a hospital for you.

Tombstone of Anicius Ingenuus, medicus ordinarius of the 1st Cohort of Tungrians. Housesteads, Nd. Sandstone. 3rd century AD. 1822.16.

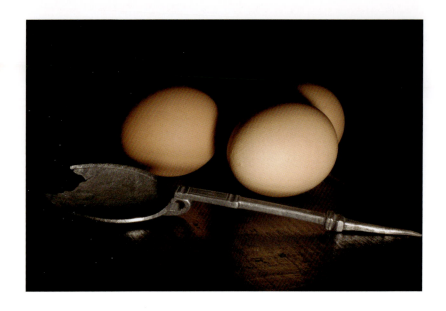

Spoon. Benwell, T&W. Silver. 2nd century AD. 1926.23.1.

Silver Spoon

Anicius, I think the spoon is yours.
It's just the sort of thing that you might own.

A wooden splinter wouldn't do for you,
nothing less than silver; you're freeborn.

And why not, for the doctor on the Wall,
who earned the honour of centurion.

I see you with a bowl of British oysters;
I see them slipping slowly from your spoon,

but what I just can't get my head around
is the thought that you would use the rat-tail end

to prick with holes the shells of eggs and snails
to stop the wicked witches coming in.

It wasn't spirits' evil that you feared
but rather that of man to fellow man.

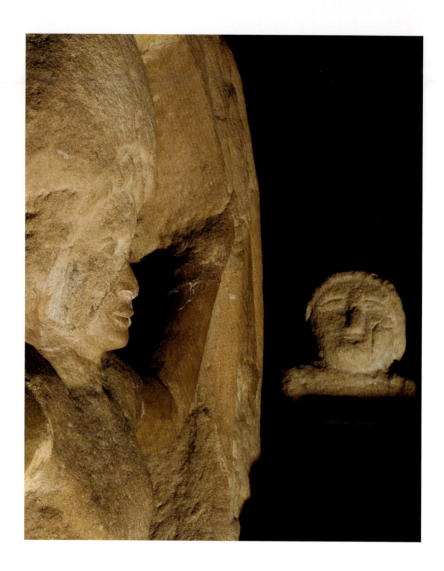

Mother goddess statue. Carrawburgh Mithraeum, Nd. Sandstone.
3rd century AD. 1956.10.27. Photographed with Birth of Mithras relief.
Housesteads Mithraeum, Nd. Sandstone. 3rd century AD. 1822.41.

A Message from the Neglected Mother Goddess to Mithras

You cracked the cosmic egg, this universe
and surrounded by the stars your light shone through.
Not to kill the bull would make things worse,
you grabbed life by the horns and claimed your due.

So, all the stars are twinkling thanks to you!
An upturned torch of hope is all you see.
No horns of a dilemma; you claimed your due.
A down-turned torch of sorrows left for me.

Your hopeful flame is plain for all to see.
I'm resting in a corner in the dark.
The dimming torch of sorrow's left with me –
the scorpion sting, the snake bite and the bark.

But in my little corner in the dark
I have no need for blood, it makes things worse.
Who needs it when I've sting and bite and bark?
Who laid this cosmic egg, this universe?

Candlestick. Carrawburgh Mithraeum, Nd. Iron. 3rd century AD. 1956.10.18.

Candlestick

He's deep inside a lonely darkened pit
and every breath he takes becomes an ordeal.
The coldness of the place has cracked his lips.
To smile is painful.

When heat returns it burns him without warming.
No torch is raised in hope nor dropped in sorrow.
He sees no rising sun and no sun setting.
Raven tomorrow.

But when he changes views a narrow sliver
of light breaks through a stone as though the sun
whipped into shape by God is told *deliver*
illumination

　　　　　on three stout legs. Enlighten this soldier –
catch his waxen teardrops in your saucer.

Seal of Approval (from a local girl)

Is this how you see yourself, hand on hip;
the hunter-gatherer flashing your knees;
a little off-the-shoulder number? Oh please,
you're a Roman citizen, get a grip!

You'll need more than a hunting-stick to hook me.
If you want to make an impression, think gold.
Don't bring me dead hares, they leave me cold;
even in the name of synchronicity.

You mustn't believe everything you see
pictured on intaglios and stones.
It's the imagists again, making free
with Silvanus, turning you into clones.
Take for your seal, the head of Mercury.
Remember the Empire in your bones.

Intaglio of Silvanus Cocidius. South Shields, T&W. Jasper.
2nd – 3rd century AD. 1962.12.

Good Luck Sign

Confronted by the sign of light on stones
you shudder. The wicked connotation
turns your stomach. (We have an inclination
to recoil from the evil in our bones.)
See rather a chariot wheel, and hear the groans
of Apollo. Use your imagination.
His coach, heavy with sunshine, is an invitation
to another day. An image like that hones
the view. So, what's before you now is a wheel
of fortune. Pretend you're a soldier;
that you've just been kissed; given the seal
of approval. You'd be grateful to hold her;
glad to cling onto the hope she makes you feel
as she pins the good luck charm on your shoulder.

Swastika brooch. Benwell, T&W. Bronze. 2nd – 3rd century AD.
1926.23.3. Background: altar to the Genius and the Standards of
the First Loyal Cohort of Vardulli. High Rochester, Nd. Sandstone.
3rd century AD. 1958.16.N.

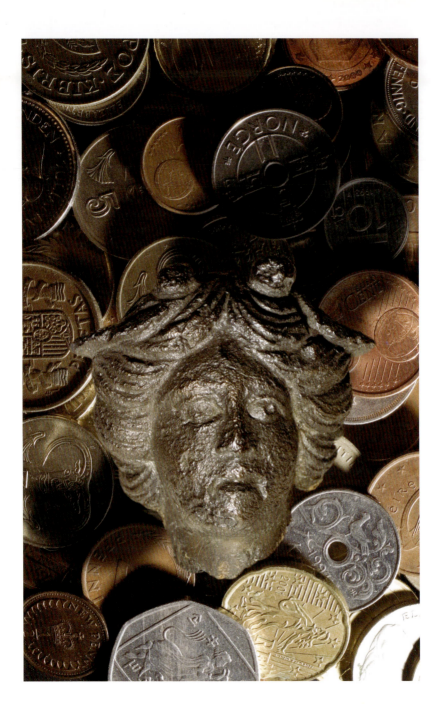

Mercury, God of Merchants

Open-mouthed you're just about to speak
and drop some god-sent snippet in our ear,
when herald duties, dumbed by rising fear,
tie your silver tongue and make it weak.
Too weak to talk with men when all they seek
is trade at any price, however dear.

You watch outside our door, but now it's clear
you're frightened for our future it's so bleak.
You hang your winged shoes up inside their case
and grieve to see us totally bereft
of decency, by making every space
a battle-ground, a killing-field for theft.

And last you chop your feet off; save your face.
You have no dreams to bring; just nightmares left.

Head of Mercury. Benwell, T&W. Bronze. 2nd – 3rd century AD. 1956.5.1.

Aemilia Finger Ring. Corbridge, Nd. Gold. 2nd – 4th century AD. 1991.1.

Aemilia and the Ring

Pure and good as gold, he picked you out
to have your tiny finger ringed with love.
He swept you off your feet, you didn't doubt
the oath he made by all the gods above.

So with your tiny finger ringed in love
you set about your duties as a wife.
That oath he made by all the gods above
provided deeper meaning in your life.

Attending to your duties as a wife
you walked beside him, closely by his arm.
And adding extra meaning to your life
gave Polemius a thicker, wider charm.

He loved it when you linked him, arm in arm.
He'd swept you off your feet without a doubt.
The charm he gave you kept you out of harm.
Pure and good as gold he'd picked it out.

Head of Minerva. South Shields, T&W. Bronze. 2nd – 3rd century AD.
1956.128.79. Background: Weaving heddle. Hardanger, Norway. Wood.
18th century AD. 1956.226.

Prayer to Minerva

To you, the reincarnation of intelligence,
I pray, please weave me some wisdom.
I too was born from the head of a great man.
Let me grow owl-faced with the years, like him.
I'm tired of being forever armed and helmeted;
of battles come from irrational posturing.
I'm wearied by having to soak my soft spots
until they become as tough as goatskin.

The reflection I make has become unattractive.
My mouth is down-turned. I find my own song
distorts my face; makes wrinkles in my forehead.
I'm worn down from being permanently strong.
Whereas you're so sure-footed in your decisions;
think nothing of reducing your enemies to spiders.

When you freed a man from his trapped love,
when you helped build ships and wooden horses,
did you never wonder whether it was worth it?
Please, Minerva, give me the gift of foresight.
Teach me when it's best to give in,
when it's best to fight.

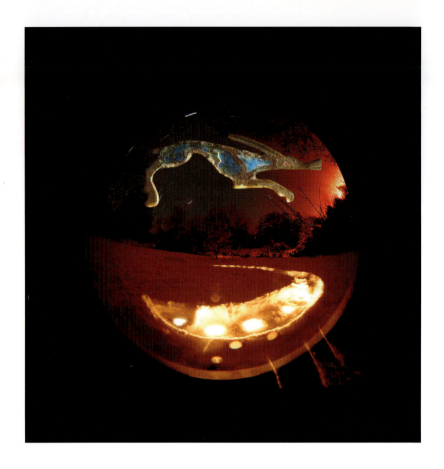

Hare brooch. Hadrian's Wall. Bronze and enamel. 2nd century AD. 1956.365

Barren

Last night, for a moment, he shone.
I thought I saw him run across the moon.
I took it as a good-luck sign,
a reward because I'd eaten hare
every ninth day and prayed to Juno
and remembered to recline
by the crackling fire after we made love.
But this morning my blood runs cold;
again. There are shivers down my spine
as women cradle bundles to their breasts.
What a disappointment I must be;
what a failure in the eyes of my fine
figure of a legionary husband,
who soldiers on in this desolate place,
where all the emptiness is mine.

Figurine of a priestess. South Shields. T&W. Bronze. 2nd – 3rd century AD. 1929.114.

Priestess

Everything is blurred
by an enigmatic smile.
The sacrifice, veiled.

Rock Wedge

In dawn mist blown from Chesters
he hews the stone; the sun's not out,
yet already his skin is glistening.

He tightens his grip round the wedge,
and frightened by the thought
of splinters, checks the feathering

that will save his face. I save mine
by hiding, in case he sees me
delight too much in tautened muscles.

He mustn't finish his section of the wall.
For many sleepless nights all I've imagined
is the width of his hand span,

the roughness of his fingers linked
with mine. His sound lingers in the air;
iron on iron, in search of fault lines.

See how repeated blows to the wedge
have crazed its head. Suppose I tell you,
as I make for Brunton Turret, mine's crazed too.

Rock wedge. Brunton Bank, Nd. Iron. 2nd century AD. 1957.5.

Figurine of Hercules. South Shields, T&W. Bronze. 2nd – 3rd century AD. 1929.113.1.

South Shields God

Like most men of Shields he loves clubbing,
chasing daughters of night beyond dusk.
It's a madness that frees him from labours,
a kind of apple-lust.

On the pull and undressed-down to kill
he's out on the town with a vengeance;
two pints and he struts like a lion;
wears the skin on his sleeve.

And if his right arm's raised in passion
it's not that he's waiting to strike.
Travolta-slim hips on the wriggle;
that's the action he seeks.

He's more of a god than a hero
to whole legions of men in the north.
The sight of him makes every woman
fall in praise at his feats.

They see past his hard reputation,
past the belt-grabbing lover of ale
to a disarmed man who would travel
the far ends of the earth.

Look again at the Shields man, the god;
test his metal against other men.
Then tell me who *you'd* rather ride with,
in the bowl of the sun.

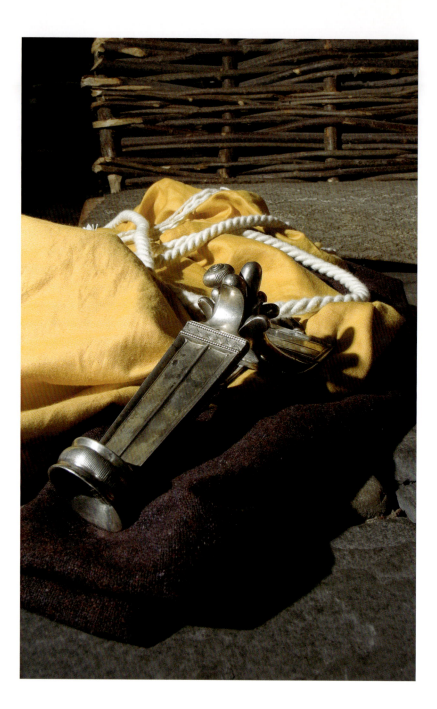

Silver Trumpet Brooch

A serious brooch needs a serious man.
I don't mean a man with no sense of humour.
I was thinking more physically serious.
His shoulders, for instance,
they'd be broad; and his chest swarthy.
Are you getting the picture?

You couldn't use a brooch like this
to pin the cloak of a puny-chested type,
his legs would buckle under the weight.
No, the legs that plant themselves, feet apart,
round the campfire, in my mind,
would be strong with hard calves.

Such a man wouldn't be from these parts,
but from somewhere strange. He'd be dark
and tall. He'd have dangerous eyes
and the waist of a woman.
Are you keeping up?

There wouldn't be an ounce of fat on him;
and if you ran up against him,
it would be like running into a stone wall.

Brooch. Great Chesters, Nd. Silver. 2nd century AD. 156.150.20.4.

Relief of a Hamian Archer. Housesteads, Nd. Sandstone. Late 2nd /early 3rd century AD. 1822.6.

Unnamed Hamian Archer

Syrian, with your unmanly, rounded shoulders,
when you became a twenty-five-year auxiliary,
gained citizen rights, left your sun-drenched valley,
did you reckon on Britain's frozen north?

When you braced your re-curve, shot over the tortoise,
did you remember to protect your arm from the string?
The way you hold yourself, the lack of bruising,
suggests you knew to bend your bowing elbow.

And when you came, one among five hundred,
were you proud to be part of the First Cohort,
or was it a bronze diploma, with its Forum duplicate
that urged you on, made you pick off the enemy?

Tell me, did you ever get that close to a barbarian,
that close, as to see the whites of his eyes?
Did you ever draw your bird-head dagger that lies
now safely back in its scabbard?

Your tight lips, your dimpled chin,
say nothing of this little Syrian.

Dice shaker and gaming pieces. Housesteads, Nd. Wood, bone and glass.
3rd century AD. 1930.44. Background: gaming board. Milecastle 9
(Chapel House), T&W. Sandstone. 3rd century AD. 1930.44.

The Blue Counters

in Ludus Latrunculorum

Sometimes there are lines drawn in the dust,
a set piece, when we square each other up.
Carefully, we place our men in twos.
The gentleman's agreement that exists
means neither of us takes the other out.

When finally our troops are all exposed
we ride on in like two blue-blooded kings
to command manoeuvres, always angling right,
one slow and painful section at a time,
to show the bloody game is all but done.

And while we penetrate the enemy line
by jumping into empty safer spaces,
our men are gutted, taken prisoner;
casualties occur on either side.
To be expected; it's a dicey game.

But it's simple; after block and counter-block,
who has the more troops standing, that man wins.

Hair comb. South Shields, T&W. Bone. 2nd century AD. 1956.128.35.

DNA

Our shadows settle quietly on the bone
and young men's secrets caught between the teeth
are mirrored thoughts they never wholly own.
Their future history set in dark relief.

As young men clench their secrets in their teeth
and find themselves backed up against a wall
their future history gives us dark relief.
We knew that much before the lads could crawl.

We see them all backed up against a wall
held firmly by a helix to their roots.
We knew before the lads could even crawl
they'd have no choice but fill their fathers' boots.

A helix holds them firmly to their roots
and mirrored thoughts are never quite their own.
They have no choice but fill their fathers' boots
as shadows settle quietly on the bone.

Towards the End

When you dropped your shield
was it because it was arrow-laden,
too heavy for its purpose?

Or were you simply tired of fighting?
Had you had enough of crawling round your empire
like a demented tortoise?

And the wounds you sustained,
were they heart-felt or merely flesh-deep,
nothing more than pride bruised?

Were you thinking, anyway, of changing sides
when your emperor called you back?
Is that why you lost your battle-nose?

Maybe thoughts of home distracted you.
Maybe you saw the writing on the wall
realised that in the end, you'd lose.

Facsimile of shield boss. R.Tyne, Herd Sands. Bronze and tin.
2nd century AD. BM. 93.12-13.1.

Gofannon

You're far too narrow-shouldered for me.
Those puny arms could not have polished ore
into shining shields. Surely you couldn't be
the Divine-Smith in charge of furnaces, or
responsible for the blades and spears of war.

You're in the right place, though, up here;
we have a tendency to play with fire.
And like you, we're stronger than we appear.
Believe me, even the scrawny ones have wire
in their blood. It takes a lot to tire

us out or wear us down; not losing ships
or closing pits. Such hardship merely hones
our wits, and looking at your tight lips
there's the same steeliness. No sticks or stones
can hurt us. Iron runs through our bones.

Figurine of smith god. Fulwell, Sunderland, T&W. Bronze.
2nd – 3rd century AD. 1956.235.

Relief of Fortuna. R. Tyne, Newcastle upon Tyne. Sandstone. 3rd century AD. 1884.12.

Fortuna

Your wings
are still buried
in our muddy river
yet you offer, with your right hand,
a drink.

Top up
every barrel,
daughter of Jupiter.
We owe our rough times and our smooth
to you.

So cheers!
Our Geordie cups
will always be half-full
not half-empty: that's our nature.
Good health.

Who knows
the stone's story
or what blessings it brought,
but we are the inheritors.
Our thanks,

Fortune,
you smiled on us.
First angel of the North,
from your horn of plenty you filled
the Tyne.

Maureen Almond

Since she began writing poetry seriously in 1992, Maureen Almond has published *Hot* (1997), *Tailor Tacks* (1999), *Oyster Baby* (2002), *The Works* (2004) and *Tongues in Trees* (2005). She has a strong interest in classical literature and is currently a research student at the University of Newcastle concentrating on the Roman poet, Horace. Her work is included in the Primary Texts Reading List for the Oxford University Course, 'The Reception of Classical Literature in Twentieth-Century Poetry in English' and has been cited in *The Cambridge Companion to Horace* (2007). She recently recorded a programme about Horace for BBC Radio 3 as part of a series dealing with his poetry. She is also a contributor in the forthcoming OUP *Living Classics: Greece and Rome in Contemporary Poetry in English.*

Glyn Goodrick

Glyn Goodrick has been working in archaeology since 1984, initially as a field archaeologist, excavating his way around England and South America. For the last twelve years, whilst working for the Museum of Antiquities, he has specialised in the interpretation and communication of archaeology through the media of photography, video, virtual reality and the internet. His interests extend beyond the confines of archaeology, and for three years he has acted as photographer-in-residence for the Buddhafield Festival, exploring aspects of interconnection, conditionality and attachment.